WHO WAS JESUS, REALLY?

Book Three

(My Bible Story Series)

JAMES TAIWO

INTRODUCTION

Hasn't it been an interesting journey so far? The *Who Is Jesus, Really?* books one and two opened our minds to better understand who Jesus was and is, how he spread God's word on Earth, and to see some of the miracles he performed.

We learned new things, thought about some of his teachings and put some things into action. In this final book, we will consider other ideas that are great blessings to children and everyone, really. Be sure to read all three books to really get to know Jesus and to learn to live like he did. Invite your friends to read the books with you and discuss each story, what you learned, and how to apply it to your life. Some of your friends might not think it's "cool" to read about Jesus, but guess what? *Cool* is what you make it. *Cool* is being brave enough to be yourself and be confident in your beliefs. *You* be the leader among your friends. *You* decide what is cool and what isn't.

Read with me as we look into the issues of obedience, love and forgiveness.

Chapter One

JESUS TEACHES US ABOUT OBEDIENCE

The Story of the Two Sons (Matthew 21, Matthew 7, John 14)

When Jesus came and performed all his miracles, getting the attention of the people, the Jewish priests and elders envied him and questioned him. They came to accost Jesus, asking him on whose authority he was doing all he did. Knowing that the Jews saw themselves as the best people, he knew they considered themselves to be holy. Jesus asked them a question to answer their question.

"The baptism of John—is it from heaven or from man?" They believed the ministry of John the Baptist; they knew he was from God. That meant they had to believe it when John said Jesus was the Lamb of God.

The elders knew that if they said, "Yes, John is from God, from heaven, Jesus would ask why they didn't believe that he, too, came from God if John said he did, and they said they didn't know.

Jesus, in his wisdom, said he would not tell them on whose authority he spoke and did these acts, but he would tell them a story:

There was a man who had two sons. He called the first son, and he came. He said, "Son, go and work in my vineyard today," but the son said, "I will not." Later, he felt bad that he disobeyed his father and decided to go and do the work.

The second son was called after the first refused the father, and he said the same thing. The second son was eager to please his father and be seen as the good son, even though he had other plans. He said, "I will go, sir," but he did not go.

Jesus then asked the elders, "Which of the two did the will of the father?" The first one, who had refused but repented, was the obedient one. So it is in Gods kingdom: those who we call sinners, the gangsters, the thieves, the bad guys, would repent and be saved.

Those who consider themselves holy and look down on others might call him Lord with their lips, but their heart is far from him. Those people would be last. The first shall be the last, and the last shall be the first.

The kingdom belongs to those who do the will of the father, not those who just call him Lord and do things to impress him, but those who obey his word and do as he says.

The proof of your love for Jesus is in obeying his commandments. Jesus said "He that has my commandments and keeps them, he it is who loves me; he who loves me shall be loved of my father. I will love him, and will manifest myself to him." How great is that promise? In the next chapter, we will talk more about love.

Think About It

Did you like *The Lord of the Rings*? Although magic appears in the story (see Book Two for a discussion of the REAL magic—God's love), it is basically about how love, obedience, self-lessness and loyalty will always conquer evil. Think about the characters in the books, or the movies, if you saw them. Which characters are selfless and do what is needed to fight evil? Which characters sacrifice themselves to do what is right? Can you think of characters who talk like they are on the side of goodness but are really following evil in their hearts? Think about the story Jesus told above. What classification do you fall under? Are you like the second son, who said yes and still did as he liked? Or are you like the first, who didn't feel like going but repented and decided to go? I want you to be like Jesus, who said yes to his father to come and die and, even when he REALLY didn't feel like dying, he said, "Not my will, but your will be done." Now, that is a perfect example of obedience. Jesus was obedient to the end, even till his death on the cross. What sacrifices are you making to be obedient?

*L*esson Learned

There is more to obedience. Your love for God compels you to do his will and, when you do his will, Jesus will be your hand as you do great things.

*T*ake Action

Whenever you say, "I love Jesus," make sure you are not just saying it. The proof of your love for Jesus is to obey and do what God has sent you to do, so that on the last day, Jesus will welcome you into the kingdom of God with open arms and not kick you down to the other place!.

. . .

Seeking Answers...

1. How can you get better at obedience?
2. What are the benefits of obedience?
3. Think about the characters in *The Lord of the Rings* and discuss why obedience was important in that story. (Frodo was a little hobbit; he was not strong, or good at fighting. He was not what we think of as a superhero. Yet he saved everyone because his heart was true. He forgave Gollum, who was pretty mean to him and his uncle.)
4. What other books or movies can you think of that are about good versus evil and one ordinary character who is chosen to fight for good?

Chapter Two

JESUS TEACHES US ABOUT LOVE

The Story of a Man that Wouldn't Forgive (Matthew 18)

*J*esus our lord is serious when it comes to the issue of forgiveness. There is no way we can express love without the heart of forgiveness. Jesus was teaching about forgiveness, and he said, "If your brother trespasses against you, tell him, and if he doesn't listen, tell it to one or two others who can settle the case, and if he still won't listen, take him to the church."

This means Jesus wants us to go all the way in trying to reconcile with someone who has offended us. He wants us to love each other and be at peace with each other, because prayers will not be answered when there is discord in our hearts.

Jesus said, "Whatsoever you bind on earth shall be bound in heaven, whatsoever you loose on earth shall be loosed in heaven. Again, I say, if two of you shall agree on earth as touching anything that they shall ask, it shall be done for them of my father, which is in heaven."

I know some of the old-fashioned words might not make sense, but that is a powerful promise right there! It means, when we live in peace, we can join hands with our friends and pray for something, and God will be happy to answer us.

Jesus went further in talking about forgiveness. He told a story, saying, "The kingdom of heaven is likened to a king, who was taking account of his servants. When he started this, one owed the king ten thousand talents. The king was furious and commanded them to sell him, his wife and his children to be able to pay back the money he owed .

"The servant fell down and worshipped the king, begging him to have patience with him, promising to pay. The king of the servants was moved with compassion and forgave him his debt. He told him he was free to go without paying the money.

"The servant was happy, but as he went out, he found one of his fellow servants who owed him a hundred pence. He caught him by the throat and asked him for his money. The fellow servant begged for more time to pay up, but the first servant would not listen.

"Other servants, who had seen how the king had forgiven him his debt and how he couldn't forgive his fellow servant, went to report the matter to the king. The king was furious with him, saying, "You wicked servant, I forgave you all your debt but you cannot forgive your fellow servant."

He was given to the tormentors, who dealt with him till he paid up every dime he owed the king.

Think About It

Have you behaved like that wicked servant lately? Do you expect your parents to forgive you but you won't forgive them, or do you hold grudges against your friends and family? God expects us to forgive others just as he has forgiven us.

It may be difficult (doing the right thing is almost always hard— look what Frodo had endure!), but you can ask God for the grace to forgive (although Gollum did some pretty heinous things, Frodo was merciful and forgave him). Would you like your unforgiveness to stop your prayers from being answered? Probably not. Be forgiving.

Take Action

Reach out to those who have offended you and try to make peace with them. Go to those you have offended and apologize. Tell them you are sorry, and let peace continue to reign.

Lesson Learned

Do unto others what you want them to do to you. Do you desire to be forgiven when you commit an offense? You should be ready to forgive others also when they offend you.

Seeking Answers...

1. Is forgiveness an easy thing to do?
2. Discuss how you can live free of offenses and grudges.

Chapter Three

JESUS TEACHES US ABOUT HELPING OTHERS

The Story of a Good Samaritan (Luke 10)

A lawyer once asked Jesus what he could do to be saved, and Jesus asked him, "What is written in the law, what do you read?"

The lawyer answered boldly, "You shall love the Lord your God with all your heart, and with all your soul and with all your strength, and with all your mind, and your neighbor as yourself."

"Bravo! You have answered right; do this and you will live," Jesus answered, but the lawyer was trying to justify his ill behavior toward someone. He asked Jesus, "Who is my neighbor?"

Jesus then told a story to answer this question.

"A man went down from Jerusalem to Jericho, and fell among thieves, who stripped him of his clothes and wounded him; they beat him and left him half dead on the road.

"Then, there came a priest passing that road, he saw the half-dead man; instead of helping him, he turned the other way.

"Then came a Levite; he got to where the man laid helpless, took a good look at him, and passed by the other side.

"There also came a certain Samaritan; as he journeyed, he came to where this man was and saw him. He had pity on him. He went to him, dressed his wounds, pouring oil and wine, and set him on his donkey. He brought him to an inn so they could take care of him, and he paid the bill."

Jesus then asked, "Who do you think was a neighbor to the man that fell in the hands of the thieves?"

The lawyer answered, "He that showed him mercy."

Jesus said, "Go and do likewise."

Think About It

How many times have you seen someone in need but ignored them or went the other way so as not to be bothered?

Would you help if you saw someone who had fallen down or had been badly wounded, or would you prefer to take pictures and put it on Facebook and laugh at him with your friends? Again, do unto others as you would have them do unto you. If you fell in the school cafeteria and dropped a whole tray of food, would you want everyone to laugh and ignore you?

Take Action

Look out for others and be willing to help, as Jesus instructed. Do not close your eyes to people's needs. You may just be a kid and, in many situations, you can't help, but if you see someone badly wounded, you can go and report it to an adult who can get help. If that person is helped, God will be happy with you for saving a life. It's hard sometimes to tell if someone is asking for money on the street whether they are really in need or just scamming. It doesn't really matter, though. If you can give a quarter to someone, does it matter if they are on the level? God will take care of that part. The only time you should not help someone is if it would put you in personal danger. Tell an adult, and let God help in that situation.

Lesson Learned

Jesus is the Good Samaritan who did not abandon us to die in sin but left everything he loved and paid the ultimate price to save us. How have you shown the light of Jesus in your neighborhood?

Seeking Answers...

1. In this generation, is it easy to want to help others when you know you might be asked to write a statement. Do you still want to help others even if no one notices?
2. Do you know that God desires that we help those in need and he is willing to protect and defend us?
3. How have you been a Good Samaritan to those around you?

Chapter Four

THE STORY OF THE SHEEP AND THE GOATS

(MATTHEW 25)

*J*esus gave one of his parables in this manner: He said, "When the son of man shall come in his glory, and all his angels with him, then he shall sit upon the throne of the kingdom of God.

"Then, all nations shall be gathered before him and he shall separate the one from another, as a shepherd divides the sheep from the goats.

"The sheep will be on his right hand and the goats on his left.

"He shall say to those on his right hand, 'Come, you blessed of my father, inherit the kingdom prepared for you from the foundation of the world. For I was hungry and you fed me, I was thirsty, you gave me drink, I was a stranger, you took me in, I was naked, you clothed me, I was sick, and you visited me, I was in prison, you came unto me.'

"The righteous on the right hand were surprised and asked Jesus, 'When did we see you hungry, thirsty, naked, sick and in prison?' And the king answered with a smile.

"'In as much as you have done to the least of my brothers, you have done to me.'"

Jesus was saying that when we show love to our fellow people, we have showed love to him. This means that when we help others, we are indirectly showing our love for Jesus.

"To the other side, Jesus said, 'Depart from me, ye cursed, into everlasting fire, prepared for the devil and his angels, for I was hungry, thirsty, naked, sick and in prison, and you neglected me."

They, too, were shocked. They had not seen the lord in any of those horrible conditions! How could the lord be hungry? If they had seen him, they would surely have helped him, but the Lord was angry with them and said that as long as it was not done to the least of his brethren, they have not done it for him.

He led them into everlasting punishment and the righteous into eternal life.

Think About It

Why would Jesus equate helping others with being righteous and being in his kingdom when he comes?

Even if we say we are children of God, if we do not have love in our heart, love for people, share what we have, our food, drinks, and clothes, and visit and care for one another, we may not see the kingdom of heaven.

You may not see Jesus physically, but he is with you and in every one of his children. If one of his children is hungry and comes to you, who have enough food, or at least a little you can spare, but refuse to, Jesus will not be happy with you.

It is important to note that you can't claim to love people and then not give to them or help them. For God so loved the world that he GAVE! He gave us the beautiful wondrous universe we live in. He gave us all we need to thrive and live. He gave us his *only son*! Surely, we can give a little of ourselves to those in need.

ake Action

Consider whether you are a sheep or a goat according to the explanation Jesus gave. If you are a sheep, keep up the good work! If you are a goat, ask Jesus to forgive you, and then ask for the grace to love and be a cheerful giver.

esson Learned

You can either be a goat or a sheep; when it comes to God, it is not safe to be on the fence. God doesn't agree with being nice today and bad tomorrow, or showing you are nice on the outside but thinking bad things inside your heart. God wants you to show love genuinely, to give and help those in need, for as long as you do this to those around you, you are doing it to Jesus.

eeking Answers...

1. Do you share your food, water and clothes with those that have nothing, or do you prefer to hold on to everything, even if you are running out of space to keep it all and you are obviously not using those things anymore?

2. Check your life. If Jesus was to come and pass judgment, would you be a sheep or a goat?

Chapter Five

WHO IS THE GREATEST?

(MATTHEW 18)

The disciples came to Jesus one day with a question. "Who is the greatest in the kingdom of heaven?"

Jesus called a little child and held the child as he taught.

"Except you be converted and become as little children, you shall not enter into the kingdom of heaven. Wherefore, whosoever shall humble himself like this little child, the same is the greatest in the kingdom of heaven."

That's pretty cool, right? Jesus said only those who become like little children (or hobbits) will enter the kingdom of heaven. Children are so adorable, and they are quick to forgive and forget. A child might have been yelled at by her mom one minute and the next, the child is running back to her mother with her arms open wide for a big hug. She is not like an adult, who would hold onto a grudge for so long and not ever talk to her mother again.

Jesus said a little child would humble himself. The greatest in the kingdom of heaven is the person who is humble and is not proud or boastful.

Are you known to be proud? Are you full of yourself, thinking you are better than other people? Maybe you should think about becoming like a child.

You may say, "But I am still a child." Well, even if you are a child physically, but you behave like you are too cool for school, then Jesus is asking you to humble yourself so that you can become truly great.

Think About It

The things people consider to be great are way different from what Jesus considers to be great. In the light of God's word, do you see yourself as great? Do you brag a lot about how good you are at video games or sports or singing? There is nothing wrong with being confident in your talents and abilities. In fact, God wants you to use your talents. Just make sure you are not walking around telling everybody how great you are all the time. Let your talents speak for themselves. All the better, use your talents in God's name!

Pride goes before a fall: therefore, beware. Like a famous person being mean to a fan: he won't be famous for long!

Take Action

Examine your actions and consider your attitude. Are

you being rude and disrespectful to your elders? Are you a know-it-all? Ask Jesus to help you be like the little child who is humble, because that is how you will become known for greatness.

*L*esson Learned

Jesus loves little children, and he says to them, "Come to me!" That sounds pretty good to me. You should say, "Thank you, Jesus, for loving me!"

*S*eeking Answers...

What are some human measures of greatness that are different from what Jesus is talking about?

Chapter Six

HE WHO IS WITHOUT SIN SHOULD CAST THE FIRST STONE

(John 8)

*J*esus went to the temple at the Mount of Olives early in the morning, and the people gathered around him as usual as he taught them the word of God.

The Scribes and Pharisees brought a woman who had been caught in adultery, messing around with a man who was not her husband. They brought her to Jesus so he could condemn her, just as they were.

As holy as the Lord was—after all, he preached holiness and living a righteous life—they figured they would test him. They had been looking for different ways to make Jesus fall into a trap and prove he wasn't the son of God. They were sure he would not escape it this time, but Jesus, of course, already knew their hearts.

They said, "Moses in the law commanded us to stone such a

woman to death. What do you say?"

Jesus knelt down and started to write on the ground with his fingers. He didn't feel pressured; he didn't even try to impress them, because he knew they were using her as a trap to set him up.

They continued to ask his opinion when they saw that he paid no attention to them. When he stood up, he made a profound statement. "He among you that is without sin, let him cast the first stone."

Wow! Totally wise. I know you, too, must be thrilled with such an answer. Jesus didn't think they had the right to condemn the woman just because she was caught. A thief might be considered a good person by everyone till the day he is caught in the act.

Jesus knew every single one of them had secret sins, but they were yet to be caught, so they pretended they were righteous and decided they could pass judgment on the woman.

Also, some probably felt her sin was greater than theirs—after all, they were not cheating on their wives. Maybe they only told lies or they only cheated on a test. Some might have harbored serious sins but, again, had not been caught. They felt justified enough to present her to Jesus. Sometimes those who are guilty of a sin condemn the very same sin in others. The bottom line is that it is not up to us to judge others. That's God's job.

When Jesus spoke, they saw themselves for who they were and the eldest person dropped his stone and walked away. One after the other, they dropped their stones. Jesus was still writing in the sand and when he raised his head, the accusers were gone.

Isn't that amazing? They were gone, meaning no one who accused the woman was free from guilt, none of them were righteous enough to want to condemn her, for all have sinned and fallen short in the sight of God.

She was left with her savior, the one who loved her and was willing to forgive her and give her a new life. Jesus said to her, "Neither do I condemn you. Go and sin no more."

Wow! That's humbling. Jesus forgave her totally and asked her to go and sin no more. This shows that it is not that Jesus liked the fact that she sinned, but that he knew there was a better way to help her than to condemn her. He made her see his love for her and gave her a responsibility to live a good and righteous life. In doing this for her, he also taught a lesson to the crowd about forgiveness and how important it is to look at yourself before you go around blaming and accusing others.

Jesus said, "I am the light of the world, he that follow me shall not walk in darkness but shall have the light of life."

The light of the life of Jesus shone on that woman when he forgave her and saved her from all her accusers. He took away reproach and told her to go and live a decent life that is pleasing to God.

Imagine how many times we have sinned against God, and still he forgives us. It is now our duty to live up to our part of the bargain and sin no more. May the Lord continue to help us and cause his glorious light to shine upon us in Jesus' name.

Think About It

Do you still see such love being portrayed in the body of Christ today? When someone errs, our first response shouldn't be to condemn because, let's be honest, we know we're not without sin and we too need the forgiveness of God. Therefore, we need to show the love of God and help the person who has sinned and not break him even more by insulting and calling him bad names, especially when he is willing to repent.

. . .

Take Action

Repent from the sin of being a judge (unless you're Aaron Judge!). The word says, "Judge not, or you might be judged." Then ask Jesus to fill your heart with love for the lost people, so you can reach out to them and bring them into the light of Jesus' life.

From now on, decide never to join anyone in mocking or condemning anybody. Imagine if Jesus were to appear and command, "Let he who is without sin cast the first stone." Would you still be bold enough to accuse?

Lesson Learned

Judge not so that you will not be judged. Show love to the lost, don't be too hard on them, and preach the grace and love of God so that they can go and sin no more.

Seeking Answers...

1. Are you the one condemning someone else, or are you the condemned?
2. Do you think you are "holier than thou" and are licensed to cast blame on everybody else?
3. Have you been mocked and condemned for sinning so that you feel God wouldn't accept a bad person like you? (Consider the response of Jesus and let his love and forgiveness comfort you. Know that God will ALWAYS accept you and give you a second chance. Just like Jesus said, "Go and sin no more.")

CONCLUSION

"You shall love the Lord your God with all your heart, with all your soul, with all your strength, and with all your mind; and love your neighbor as yourself."

Jesus taught with that commandment in mind. He wanted us to love God and do his will, and he also expected us to show our love for God in how we treat others. You cannot say you love God and hate your brother or your enemy. Who is Jesus, really? Jesus is God, and God is love; therefore, let us love just like he loved.

ABOUT THE AUTHOR

James Taiwo is the founder and senior pastor of World Outreach Evangelical Ministry in New York City. He holds a Doctor of Theology degree and a Master of Science Degree in Environmental Engineering. A practicing civil and environmental engineer and preacher, James also plays saxophone and is an avid blogger. With the aim of diversifying the gospel to adapt to the fast-changing technology of our day, he is the publisher of Trumpet Media Ministries and author of several books, including *Bible Application Lessons and Prayers*, *Book of Prayers*, *Pinnacle of Compassion*, *Christian Principle Guides*, and *Roadmap to Success*. James lives in New York City with his wife and children.

CONNECT WITH THE AUTHOR

Please add your honest, positive reviews of this book online. Rate this book five stars now at
http://bit.ly/who-jesus-3

Sign up for new book alert from the author at
www.bit.ly/bookalertme

Visit the author's website at
www.jamestaiwo.com

Connect with the author on social media

f facebook.com/jamestaiwoJT

🐦 twitter.com/theJamesTaiwo

a amazon.com/author/jamestaiwo

ALSO BY JAMES TAIWO

Bible Application Lessons and Prayers

Bible Giants of Faith

Christian Principle Guides

Book of Prayers

Who Was Jesus, Really? - Book One

Who Was Jesus, Really? - Book Two

Who Was Jesus, Really? - Book Three

Who Was Jesus, Really? - Boxset

The Pinnacle of Compassion

The Ancient Houses of Egypt

Success Express Lane (Your Roadmap To Personal Achievement)

www.ingramcontent.com/pod-product-compliance
Lightning Source LLC
Chambersburg PA
CBHW060645030426
42337CB00018B/3447